Claim Your Brilliance

50 Keys to Fearless Confidence, Visibility & Success

Lisa Meisels

Disclaimer

The purpose of this book is to educate and entertain. The author or publisher does not guarantee that anyone following the ideas, tips, suggestions, techniques or strategies will become successful. The author and publisher shall have neither liability nor responsibility to anyone with respect to any loss or damage caused, or alleged to be caused, directly or indirectly by the information contained in this book.

Claim Your Brilliance Praise

"Lisa has written a fearlessly honest and insightful guide that will help women coaches break through to new levels of visibility and success online. 'Claim Your Brilliance' is full of uplifting and actionable advice straight from the trenches -- from Lisa's own entrepreneurial journey. Get your copy and claim YOUR brilliance. I couldn't put it down!" -- Jill Hendrickson, Creator of Authors and Bestsellers. www.JillHendrickson.com

"Finally, here's the book that every entrepreneur needs to have--a personal tool kit for fixing the ups and downs we all experience in our business. Every business owner I know goes through periods where they get 'stuck', when business isn't coming in and we worry that there's some piece that they're missing. In "Claim Your Brilliance", Lisa lays out 50 beautifully written solutions for the emotional roadblocks around selling, networking and being seen as authentic, as well as brass tacks business solutions to marketing, time management and creating funnels. A must-read for entrepreneurs!" --Sally Domingo Laughlin, International Speaker & Wealth Empowerment Expert, Founder of Women Wealth Mastery. www.womenwealthmastery.com

"Lisa Meisels' book, Claim Your Brilliance, details every aspect involved in creating success in business. The information is written in a step-by-step style, concise, easy to read, and impactful. With all the many how-to books on the market, this is the one that says it all in palatable nuggets. Meisels offers encouragement in a personal way as if she is a best friend who supports, builds confidence, and shows the way to success for women in business." -- Julaina Kleist-Corwin, bestselling author of "Create Loyal Fans". www.timetowritenow.com

"Whether you are at the beginning of your journey or well into it, "Claim Your Brilliance" will guide you into a deeper connection with yourself, your message, and your audience. This deceptively small book is huge inside. It's incredibly full of valuable insights and ideas that will help you lead and inspire yourself... and others!" --Beth Bridges, The Networking Motivator and author of "Networking on Purpose". www.TheNetworkingMotivator.com

Thank-You

Hi, I'd like you to get the most out of this book, so if you haven't done so already, head over to my website and grab your free Online Visibility and Impact Checkup www.LisaMeisels.com so that we can stay in touch. This Assessment is a great tool and will show you the areas you are rocking it with your online presence and where you need to focus to become more visible.

And if you find any typos while you're reading this book, I'd love for you to let me know! Feel free to email me at lisa@lisameisels.com.

I absolutely won't take it personally. In fact, I'll be grateful to you. We're all in this together!

About the Author

Hi, I'm Lisa Meisels your Online Visibility & Impact Strategist. I work with women coaches, visionaries, thought-leaders and change-makers who've had successful careers and now feel called to be more intentional with their work, so they can enjoy life with less hustle and still make a big impact in the world.

After nearly 30 years, I left my corporate career. I discovered a new world online, but I struggled to gain traction in my online business. I didn't know how to bring all my talents, skills and unique gifts together into a message. I didn't understand how to articulate my value. I couldn't figure out who my ideal client was or where to find them. As a result, I spent years in the "spin-cycle" trying every new strategy without success. And because I was in front of the wrong audience, they didn't want to invest in my services. I felt like I was invisible online. But I also knew I couldn't fail.

I realized that I had to first peel off the sterile, professional persona I had identified with for so long. Being visible online required me to be seen and I knew I had to find myself again. I began connecting with people in a real, raw and vulnerable way. The more I shared from my heart, the more clients I attracted. I gained massive traction in my business once I discovered I could use my intuition to identify the exact ideal audience for my clients. It's funny, I used to get teased about thinking backwards. Now I utilize this quirk in my unique reverse-engineered process that drills down to the root connection between my client and their collective dream audience. This process makes it easy for my clients to find the exact solution that their audience is ready to invest in.

I believe we are here on earth to find joy through our service to others. I love working with my clients and hearing about the amazing results they've achieved. My process to get you visible, attract clients online and make an impact in the world is simple, practical and customized. Are you ready to gain visibility and influence so you can share your message, transform lives and impact the world?

Want a Great Speaker for Your Next Event?

Lisa Meisels is the Best!

To Schedule Lisa Meisels to Speak at Your Event:
Lisa@LisaMeisels.com
www.LisaMeisels.com

Dedication

To all the courageous women in the world on a journey to step up to their calling, speak their truth, claim their unique gifts and help others in service within a new model of business, so together we can shine our lights raising the vibration of the planet and doing our part to heal the world.

Why You Need to Read This Book

Have you ever wondered why you aren't getting noticed and getting consistent clients online? If you've ever experienced feelings of confusion, frustration, self-doubt or overwhelm to the point of doubting yourself for even starting an online business, you're not alone.

When I first came online, I struggled with feeling clear about my message, knowing who my ideal audience was, where to find them and feeling confident about communicating the value of my services. I couldn't figure out how to clearly articulate what I did and the results I could get people. I felt invisible as if I were hidden online. I had a hard time getting noticed by those who needed my services and I didn't know how to get clients online.

I took course after course and hired mentor after mentor and after spending many thousands of dollars, I still couldn't put the puzzle pieces together to find success- until I figured out a shortcut.

I realized it doesn't have to be as hard as all the gurus tell you. In this book, I share my discoveries with you that not many experts are willing to give away. I want to simplify the process to help you on your journey of growing an online business. A business where you feel excited and on fire every day.

If you're the kind of woman who feels the need to go, go, go and push to feel successful, but would rather slow down, feel balanced shift into flow, and find success, than this book is for you. These are the same strategies I used, and I know you'll find them of great value."

Lisa Meisels

The 50 Keys

Fearless Confidence

Fearless confidence is derived from clarity

Key # 1: Find Clarity in Your Value

I believe that we are all here on earth to share our unique brilliance with the world in service to others. Becoming an entrepreneur is a journey of self-discovery and personal healing. It's not for the faint of heart. It takes dedication and commitment. The reason people say it's "hard" is because as you build your business, you are using skills you've never used before. You're likely in uncharted waters. It requires you to level up and stretch yourself to the point of becoming more of who you're meant to be in the world.

Let's face it, you got into business for a reason. There was something inside you that clicked and made you want to start your business. You might have gone through an event that changed your life and now you want to share your discovery with the world. Maybe you're still working for "the man" and want to quit your day job. Whatever the situation, there is a reason you started a business.

To discover your value, you must be willing to go into the shadows and depths of your beingness. Each time you try something new or implement a different strategy, you will find out more about who you are. Each time you reach another milestone in your success, you will expand. Expansion requires you to face your fears, take a good look at your habits and acknowledge past patterns that have been keeping you stuck.

Fear beckons you. It calls on you so that you can level up. The only way to level up, is to move through the stuff that keeps you stuck. Most of the time, it's not strategy. What I find is that often, lack of clarity, lack of alignment and lack of joy keep you stuck. People refer to these as limiting beliefs or mindset issues. Everyone has "stuff" they must get through to discover their value. I encourage you to dig into the depths of your being and go to that place of discomfort. Go through the doors of fear to get to the other side where the magic occurs. You have value to bring the world. You just need to claim it!

Contemplation

Think for a moment. How you will you apply this in your business? Why did you get into business? What value do you bring to the world? What fears do you need to overcome to claim your brilliance? Write it down.

"Your uniqueness is your brilliance" – Lisa Meisels.

Key #2: Use Your Inner Compass

If you've ever had situations where you struggled to make things work, you got frustrated or where you just felt "off", it is probably because you were out of alignment.

When you are out of alignment, you feel stuck, confused, frustrated and exhausted. You begin to doubt yourself. You wonder if being in business for yourself is the right thing. When you feel like this, you know there is something out of alignment. It's time to get out your inner compass.

You get into alignment by feeling into it. Use your heart as a compass to navigate life. This is how you can feel into alignment. With an open heart, you can bypass the mind which is what keeps you stuck.

When I refer to your mind, I'm referring to your ego which wants to protect you and keep you safe. The ego originates in the primitive brain. You may be cognitively aware that a fear is not related to survival in life however, the same feelings occur when the ego senses any kind of fear.

When you are in alignment, you don't have to try hard. You don't feel like you're pushing to make things work. You don't feel like you are running against the wind. Instead, you feel as if you are flowing in a river of synchronicities and joy.

Use your heart instead of your mind. Follow your joy. When you are in joy, you are in alignment. You no longer will feel the need to push yourself to go, go, go. Instead, you'll feel excited about life. You will jump out of bed, exhilarated and ready for the day. You will go through your day with ease and in flow. Yes, there will still be occasional times where you get frustrated or overwhelmed. However, the joy and excitement you feel far outweighs any negative feelings.

You can easily move into alignment by spending time getting quiet every day. Feel into your heart and bypass the mind chatter. Ask your heart what it really wants. What brings you joy and excites you? When you use your inner compass, and operate from here in your business, you will feel the shift into flow. This is when you gain momentum.

Contemplation

Think for a moment. How will you apply this in your business? Spend time every day in quiet to feel into your heart. Be aware of what feels joyful and navigate life from that space. Write it down.

The more you know what you don't want, the better you can understand what you do want" – Lisa Meisels

Key # 3: Confidence Comes from Clarity

Everyone including you has a story. Often people question what part of their life they should share with their audience. We all have such rich life experiences it can be difficult to pull out exactly which one to share. However, there is exactly one part of your life that relates to your ideal audience. This is the part that you want to share.

Sharing the parts of your story that are real, raw and vulnerable will help you to connect with your audience. You want them to know that you "get" them. You want them to see that you've been where they are too. You want them to believe that they can get through their difficult times too because they see that you have.

Telling your story, the right way builds trust with your audience. The more you can relate to what your audience is going through, the more of a deep connection you will build with them. If you keep your story factual with no emotion, your audience will not feel engaged with you.

Share the part of your past that lead up to the event that changed your life. Because your audience is going through what you've been through, you will build a deep connection with them. You can then share what you did to get out of your dark place, what realizations you had that helped you propel forward and how you ultimately healed. This will help your audience recognize that it is possible for them too.

When your story connects at a deep level, you will build the know, like and trust factor that is so important in any relationship, including the one you are building with your audience.

Contemplation

Think for a moment. How will you apply this in your business? What lead up to the event that changed your life? How did you move through that time in your life? How were you feeling during this time? And how did you come out of your darkness to heal? Write it down.

"What you leave behind is not what is engraved in stone monuments, but what is woven into the lives of others."- Pericles

Key # 4: Acknowledge Your Gifts

It's common to want to cover up the parts of your life that you don't feel great about. However, it is in the dark shadows of your past, that you'll find your divinely given gifts.

There is richness in your past experiences. Sometimes people don't recognize these as gifts. They show up in life as difficulties, challenges and traumas. They are the parts of your life that are bundled in emotions of shame, guilt, sorrow, anger and grief. Don't burry these emotions. Bring them into the light.

When you begin to share these parts of your life, healing occurs for you and for those around you. These life experiences happened FOR you, not to you. They happened so that you could go through them, learn more about yourself and ultimately help others with your realizations.

People often ask me how much they should share with their audience. The key is sharing when you are on the other end of the journey having already gone through your darkness. This way, you can share from a place of love, light and understanding. If you are still stuck in the depths of the emotions from any hardships, you will not be able to share the lesson you learned or the growth within yourself that occurred. When you have gone through the darkness and are able to see it for what it really is- a gift, then it is time to share.

When I work with my clients, I show them how this part of their life is the part that is not only a gift for them, but their gift to others. I show them how their past experiences dictate exactly who their audience is and why.

You are being guided to step up to a new level in life. You are being guided to do something different, something uncomfortable and something that requires you to change. This can be scary. Many women try to hold off the feeling of being called for years. But if you do this, it will just leave you unhappy for longer.

Contemplation

Think for a moment. How will you apply this in your business? What challenges, hardships or traumas have you been through? How have these happened FOR you? What lessons have you learned? What healing has occurred? What are you willing to share? Write it down.

"If you hear a voice within you say, 'you cannot paint,' then by all means paint, and that voice will be silenced."- Vincent Van Gogh

Key # 5: Recognize Your Soul-Calling

You have a purpose here on earth. Do you know your soul-calling? The entrepreneurs that I work with have a calling to help transform lives, so they can make a bigger impact in the world. Many people call this their "soul calling" or their "purpose work".

Often my clients tell me that they feel as if they are being guided in a specific direction. This direction may seem like it came out of the blue. For instance, many women have been in a professional career all their life and they never thought about doing anything else. That is until some crisis or event occurs that cause them to wake up, smell the roses and realize they need to enjoy life now.

Often these events look like a health concern, relationship breakdown, a spiritual awakening or a change in the work environment. For me, it was 3 of the above. Management had changed and so had my work environment. I was sick all the time and it was getting worse. And during this time, I was awakening, acknowledging my spiritual gifts and healing abilities that I now get to use with my clients.

Your soul-calling or purpose work is the big work you are here to do in the world. Only you will intimately know what that is. You will feel a pulling towards something you're meant to do. You may not know what it is, or where this inner guidance is leading you, but you know for sure that you are being called to move in a specific direction.

You won't know exactly how things will come to fruition but that is not up to you. I always say, "the magic is in the unknown".

It's important to recognize your calling. Your calling is real. It is the Universe shaking you up, letting you know that you are stuck, and life could be so much more.

You always have a choice of which direction to take in your life. You can stay stuck, sick or miserable. Or you can experience joy, freedom and balance.

If you don't listen to your inner guidance which is asking you to step up into who you want to become, you will always have a nagging inside you. You could even be a successful entrepreneur but if you're not heeding the call of your soul work, you will not have the life you dream of.

Are you up for the challenge? Are you willing to be uncomfortable, so you can grow into more of the greatness that you don't yet know you are capable of? Are you tired of struggling to get out there in a bigger way? Are you frustrated with your low income? Is your energy low? These are all signs that you are not in alignment with your soul purpose.

Your purpose work can take on different shapes and forms. You can do your purpose work in a job just as well as you can when you're having a conversation with someone or building your business.

When you are not following your soul-calling, you will feel miserable. You'll be exhausted or lack energy. You will feel apathetic and unexcited about life.

When you are doing your soul-work you will feel in alignment. You will know you are living your purpose because you are in joy- enjoying every moment of your life.

The key is to let go of controlling every outcome (which is not easy) and surrender to the moment of what is. Follow the direction that tugs at your heart's desire.

Contemplation

Think for a moment. How will you apply this in your business? What is your purpose work? How does your soul-calling tug at your heart? Write it down.

"Day by day, what you choose, what you think and what you do is who you become."- Heraclitus

Key # 6: Become Fearless Through a Clear Vision

Do you have a big vision? Having a clear view of what impact, you want to make in the world helps you continuously move toward the beacon of light that is your vision.

Your vision is a snapshot of what you will find at your destination. How do you envision your business or service making the world different? What do you want to be known for? What impact do you want to make and why? These are questions you can ask yourself to define your vision. Craft your vision carefully. When done right, you will create a path that leads you forward with clarity.

I dedicated this book to my vision. It's interesting to note that although my niche has changed since I first started my business in 2010, my vision at its core, remains the same. The way I help people has shifted but the outcome of my work has not. Your vision, will be revealed in the way you show up and deliver results in your business.

Your vision is different than your mission. Your mission is the driving force behind the impact you want to have on the world. It explains how you will get to your Vision. Your mission is the strategy that inspires you and leads you forward in your business. It's usually a short, clear statement that is action-oriented and summarizes what you will do in your business now to get where you want to go. You want it to be measurable, so you can determine that you have succeeded. You want your statement to be inspirational not only for you, but for your team and potential partners. Knowing this helps you feel clear and confident.

I'm personally on a mission to inspire and empower over 5000 women in the next 5 years who are committed to transforming lives and positively impacting the world. I offer high quality, stream-lined processes and training that simplify creating a business, becoming visible as the go-to expert in their niche and generating income online.

Your mission statement is something that can be shared with your team to inform and inspire them, so you are working together towards the same goal.

Contemplation

Think for a moment. How will you apply this in your business? What is your vision and your mission? Write it down.

"We are what we repeatedly do. Excellence then, is not an act, but a habit."- Aristotle

Key # 7: A Clear Message Creates Confidence

Having a crystal-clear brand message is important! It's your virtual street-sign. It's is a culmination of who you are and what you stand for. It doesn't matter if you are selling a product or a service, branding your personal message is a MUST.

Your message is the voice of your company. It tells a story that people can get behind. It creates recognition and relatability with your audience. It addresses their biggest problem. And it provides inspiration and motivation for them. You want to stand out from your competitors. Focus on a specialty and create a sense of empowerment for your audience.

Your message is usually a culmination of challenges you've overcome that have happened in your life. It could also be a combination of past patterns, habits or mistakes that you've made in your life and you don't want others to make.

Your message can be derived from either positive or negative situations that have occurred in your life which you do or don't want other people to have to go through.

Here are some questions you can ask yourself:
- What is something you feel very passionate about that you wish others knew?
- What irks you to the point that you get very emotional?
- What do you want to be known for?
- How do you want to make others feel when they see your message?
- What do you want to take a stand for?

When you know why you're in business and your message is in alignment with your life lessons, and when you know exactly who your audience is, you lock confidence in place.

Use the brand message creator on the next page to create your message.

Contemplation

Think for a moment. How will you apply this in your business? Use this formula to create your brand message: The emotion you want to evoke with your brand + the verb you use that will get your audience to take action + the beneficial promise you make to your audience = your brand message. Write it down.

"Know how to listen and you will profit even from those who talk badly." - Plutarch

Key # 8: Be Clear on the Results You Provide

Part of feeling confident is acknowledging the results you get people when they work with you. This is the real reason experts will tell you that you need to work with a handful of one-on-one clients first, before you work with groups. It's not only to get to know your audience better, but it's to help you understand exactly what results you get for your clients.

When you can clearly articulate the results, you are able to get for your clients, you will also be able to attract those people that want the exact results you can help others achieve.

It is very important that you can clearly communicate to your audience how you can get them to their desired outcome. Remember, people don't want to know about what process you use to get them the results, they just know they want results.

How do you determine what results you can get for your clients? The best way is to look at what you are naturally good at, what people ask you for help with, and what you love to do. This combination of your life experience, skills, and what you love to do is very powerful.

I always tell my clients to make a list of at least 10 results that they can get people. When you're working with your clients, get their feedback and their perspective of the results they obtained from working with you. Always ask for their feedback. This helps you in your market research, with your copy and in sales conversations.

Contemplation

Think for a moment. How will you apply this in your business? Think of at least 10 different results that people get when they work with you. Write it down.

"Beware the barrenness of a busy life."- Socrates

Key # 9: Identify Your Dream Client

When you are clear about who it is that you want to work with, you will start to attract them. Have you ever heard of the reticular activating system? According to the dictionary, the RAS is "a diffuse network of nerve pathways in the brainstem connecting the spinal cord, cerebrum, and cerebellum, and mediating the overall level of consciousness". The RAS is responsible for hearing words you've just learned or seeing the same care you want to buy all over the place. Your brain creates a filter for what you focus on. When you choose to focus on something, you are putting out a request to the Universe to search and bring forth into existence.

Who is your dream client? I previously wrote about your gifts, past experiences and soul-calling. Who has your life set you up to work with? There is a group of people with similar characteristics and values that are your ideal client. You understand them, they trust you and you have the solution they are looking for.

Something very important to understand starting now, is to be yourself. You don't want to build a business and attract the wrong. If you are not showing up as yourself, you will attract people that you will not resonate with. Share your philosophies on life. Share your opinions and points of view. Don't be afraid to do this. This causes polarity. Be honest with yourself. Who do you like working with? And just as importantly, who do you not like working with? You want to cause polarity, so you can attract the exact people who you want to work with and who in turn, will love and adore you. You also want to repel the people you don't want to work with. Don't be afraid of polarizing. Be yourself. Be bold. Be proud of who you are.

When I first started, I was afraid to show up as myself and I had a hard time attracting my audience and getting clients. I never brought up the fact that I live on a ranch, go hiking, adventure on the property in the ATV, love animals, like to have fun, and am a little quirky. I tried to be liked by everyone. And because of that, I attracted people that didn't get me. Now, I attract my BFFs. Women I love and adore. Many of my clients become my friends because we click. That's what you want.

Contemplation

Think for a moment. How will you apply this in your business? What are your dream client's characteristics? How can you be polarizing? Write it down.

"Courage is knowing what not to fear."- Plato

Key # 10: Confidently Describe the Solution You Offer

You have a solution to your dream client's problem. Knowing how you describe your solution can make or break your business. When I first started I did not know how to talk about my services in a way that my audience understood. It left them confused and uninterested. It left me clientless.

The turning point for me was learning how to do market research. At first the term "market research" was scary. It sounded hard. But once I started doing it, I came to love it. Market research is basically asking your audience specific questions to get their perspective. You want to know how they talk about their problem and the solution they are looking for.

I remember years ago creating a beautiful program for my future clients. I spent thousands of dollars hiring a website designer and a graphic artist to get the program up on my site and make it look beautiful. I spent months working on the content until it was just perfect. When it was ready to go, I was excited. I had people sign up for a raffle and gave it away to a few people to get their feedback.

Not one of them went through the entire program. No one was even interested in it once they started going through it. I was devastated and confused. Then I began to understand where the disconnect was. I had not done my market research. I offered people a solution I thought they needed, not one that they wanted. Even though the content was good, and the site was beautiful, it did not give my audience the solution they wanted in a way that was consumable for them.

Find out how your people like to learn and give content to them in bite-size pieces. People who are looking for your solution will show up when you are able to articulate your solution in their language. Discover their language doing good market research. The key is to find out what your audience wants and give them what they need.

Contemplation

Think for a moment. How will you apply this in your business? What does your audience want? How do you describe your solution? Write it down.

"The only true wisdom is in knowing you know nothing." - Socrates

Key # 11: Don't Be Afraid to Give Your Best Ideas Away

Always give excellent value. I have heard experts tell people that they should only tell their audience what they need to know and not how to implement it. This was a trend in the industry several years back. But it has since changed.

The reason for the change is that there is an indescribable amount of information available at everyone's fingertips through the internet. People can search Google all day long and find the information they need.

That's not where people get stuck. They get stuck absorbing the information and integrating into their life or business. People have trouble taking action on what they learn. So no longer is the rule tell people the "what" and not the "how". If you follow this rule, you are certain to lose your audience to someone else who has the exact same services as you do.

Giving excellent value means giving people the steps they need in a way that they understand and will get a result. If people aren't getting results with your content, they will not stick around for long.

We live in a world of content overload. Giving excellent value means meeting your audience where they are, connecting with them in a meaningful way, giving them what they want and inspiring them to become who they want to become. Inspiration is an important and often missed ingredient to a successful business.

You are not going to gain confidence sitting behind your computer all by yourself and not interacting with your audience. Giving excellent value means being available to your audience in a way that builds the know, like and trust factor. Always give excellent value. Ask your audience what they want and give it to them. Be the expert that connects and makes people feel heard and seen. Be the leader that inspires them to level up.

Contemplation

Think for a moment. How will you apply this in your business? What can you do differently to ensure you are giving excellent value to your audience? Write it down.

"No man ever steps in the same river twice, for it's not the same river and he's not the same man."- Heraclitus

Key # 12: Peel Back Your Layers

I've written about your life experiences and how they are your gifts. These experiences also created situations that made you feel unsafe, insecure, not good enough and all those negative thoughts that nag at you when you're doing something that is leading to a breakthrough.

No matter who you are, you have built up layers of protection to keep you safe and secure. These prevent you from feeling fearless and confident. These layers often look like perfectionism, people-pleasing, professionalism and rebellion. They can also show up in your life as being highly successful, a high-achiever, having impressive credentials or multiple certifications all of which make you feel better about yourself. But they are layers of protection that you have built around yourself to hide your brilliance.

You cover up your uniqueness to blend in, be normal or fit in. I know, I'm a recovering perfectionist and people-pleaser. I spent years hiding behind my professionalism. When I first started my entrepreneurial journey, I didn't know who I was. I had lost my light. I had tried for years to be something I thought everyone else wanted me to be. I was highly successful and always did the right thing. I followed the rules. But on the inside, I felt boxed-in and trapped.

It took me years to peel back my layers. It takes some deep inner work. It takes going to those places you haven't wanted to look for a long time because they are painful. But if you want to be confident, you must get to know who you are underneath all your protection. You need to dust off the dirt and excavate the gem that you are. This is your healing journey that you must go through if you want to be successful. Shine the light in the dark, scary places and begin to heal. This does not happen overnight. It's an ongoing process which continues as you expand and reach success after success.

Contemplation

Think for a moment. How will you apply this in your business? What are some layers of protection that you can recognize? Where in your life do you feel trapped and out of alignment? What dark places do you need to shine the light on, so you can heal? Write it down.

"One of the most beautiful qualities of true friendship is to understand and to be understood."- Seneca.

Key # 13: Your Beliefs Keep You Stuck

Your beliefs can get in the way of your confidence, visibility and success. It doesn't matter what you do, or who you are, you have beliefs that do not serve you. We all do. I still do. It can take a lifetime to recognize them however, I believe that if you are on the entrepreneurial journey, you are fast-tracking your ability to move past any limiting beliefs.

Your beliefs are often manifestations of your unconscious mind. They are imbedded into your mind from past events that you had to deal with from a child-perspective. One event or situation can impact you as a child that if you were to look at as an adult, it would be meaningless. For instance, I remember when I was three years old, I asked for some ice cream for dessert. I was told no and sent to bed. I remember crying so hard that my father came in and asked me what was wrong. To me, being told I couldn't have ice cream and being sent to bed mean that my father didn't love me. As an adult, I can see clearly that not getting desert has nothing to do with love, but that was the truth for my child-self.

That feeling of not being loved got imprinted in my memory. Unfortunately, that subconscious memory has surfaced repeatedly as a recurring pattern in my adult life. The key is recognizing the beliefs and patterns for what they are- old memories that protected you for a time and that are no longer serving you.

It's time to let them go. The first step is to become aware of them. The next step is to see them for what they are- old stories. The last step is to acknowledge them and let them go free. When you're able to do this, you will notice your confidence increasing. You will notice that you no longer need to be liked and validated by everyone. You are enough just as you are. All the answers you ever needed are within you right now. You have access to them always. You just need to tap into your higher self and ask for guidance.

Contemplation

Think for a moment. How will you apply this in your business? What old stories are you telling yourself? How is this keeping you stuck your business? Write it down.

"True happiness is… to enjoy the present without anxious dependence on the future."- Seneca

Key # 14: Access Confidence Through Your Higher Self

You have access to anything you want. You are an unlimited being- a spirit in a human body. You are capable of more than you think. You've been playing small, not knowing otherwise. It's time to tune into your higher self and feel into the place where you will find all the answers.

I remember recognizing that I had all the answers within me at a very young age. I've been in tune with metaphysical philosophies since I was 15. As I went through my challenges, I had an inner knowing that I was being supported by something greater than myself.

I always knew I had the answers inside me, but I didn't know how to access them for the longest time. It's really the entrepreneurial journey that has allowed me to access my higher self any time I want. As I practice doing this, I feel more ease and flow in my life. As I take the time to tune in multiple times a day, I recognize when I am in alignment and when I need to make a subtle shift.

You may feel as if you are governed by your mind but that is simply not true. That is how society has molded you, but it doesn't have to be that way. You can step into your heart and access your higher self at any time, in any moment that you wish. You can get answers to any questions you have. You can navigate your business and life through your higher self. It takes practice. It takes consistency. And once you feel it, you'll never go back.

When you reach the place of bliss, alignment and the excitement of knowing, you become unstoppable! Any confidence issues will be resolved with clarity and knowingness.

I've created this special visualization that helps you access your higher self. You can get it here: http://bit.ly/youaremagnificent
.

Contemplation

Think for a moment. How will you apply this in your business? What will you commit to right now to make a consistent practice of accessing your higher self? Write it down.

"Be as you wish to seem". - Socrates

Key # 15: Become Fearless in Your Zone of Genius

You are different than anyone else in this entire world. That is why it doesn't work when someone tells you what business formula will work for you. You must be the one to figure that out.

You can access your zone of genius by bringing your natural talent, your passion and your skills together. Working in this zone allows you to create a business that is unique to you.

Being able to acknowledge when you're in this zone is the first step. You'll recognize it because you'll feel on fire! When you're not working in your zone of genius, you'll feel like you're forcing something to work or you're trying hard and you're not seeing results.

On the other hand, when you've located your zone of genius, you'll be excited about your business, your life, the people you work with, those around you, you'll feel abundant and prosperous.

Use your inner compass to navigate when you are working in your zone of genius and when you're not. Eventually, you can outsource all tasks that don't feel in alignment with your genius.

Contemplation

Think for a moment. How will you apply this in your business? What is your zone of genius? What are you doing when you feel unstoppable? Write it down.

"Success consists of going from failure to failure without loss of enthusiasm."- Winston Churchill

Visibility

Being Visible Requires Being Seen
Being Seen Requires Fearless Confidence

Key # 16: Step Up & Be Seen

Visibility is not the same as being seen. And this is what stops many women entrepreneurs that I know. They want to be visible but they're afraid to be seen.

Many of my clients come to me wondering why they are not getting noticed online. They are posting on different social media sites and they are posting on their blog. But they are posting information. They have not been willing to show up as who they are, be vulnerable and really be seen.

To become visible, you must show up as your unique self. This requires you to share your content on a more personal level. That is why "behind the scenes" posts are so popular. People are interested in who you are, what you do, how you operate and what you're all about. They want to know about your personality. They want to know what you like and what you don't like.

People want to be entertained. We live in a "Reality TV" life and it requires being willing to step out and be seen in all your glory- the good, the bad and the ugly.

It's easy to hide behind facts and stats but those will go unnoticed. If you want to get noticed online, you must show up and be vulnerable. Be willing to share some of your weaknesses. Be willing to share what you've been through, so your audience can connect with you. If you don't connect in a personal manner, if you don't stand out in your own brilliance, if you hide behind your perfection and professionalism, you will not get noticed. You will stay hidden and invisible to those who need you most. It's time. Be willing to step up, stand out and be seen!

Contemplation

Think for a moment. How will you apply this in your business? What can you do differently that will help you be seen? Write it down.

"Necessity is the mother of invention."- Plato

Key # 17: Fearlessly Brand Yourself

Branding is more than just your logo, company name and brand colors. Your brand is your company's vibe. It's your company's personality. Although your brand includes the logo and name, it also includes your personality as the business owner.

What vibe do you want people to recognize your business for? I want to be known as a business that inspires, provides excellent service and gets results. That means that I must show up and empower my audience and inspire them in addition to providing excellent value. I must be able to get people the results they want and that I say I can get for them to stay in integrity with my brand.

I get the question a lot "what should I name my company"? I remember asking this question when I first started out. I was told that I should create a company name because no one would be able to pronounce my last name. I also had big dreams of selling my company someday.

I made the mistake of naming my company Femanna. It was clever and meant something special to me. I put the words 'female" and "manna" together to create Femanna- the divine power within all females. The problem is, no one knows what Femanna means. No one can pronounce it, and no one has ever Googled the word Femanna.

You should always brand yourself. Either using your name as the name of your company or your personal brand message as the name of your business. I have branded my name. I've chosen my group brand "Unleash Your Mojo Online" because that's what my audience wants to be able to do. They want to be able to step up to their calling and show up as the real, raw person they are online. They want to show up with all their mojo and unleash it, so they can be authentic, feel in alignment and be able to attract the people that they want to work with and enroll those that want to work with them. That's my vibe!

Contemplation

Think for a moment. How will you apply this in your business? What is your brand vibe? How do you want to be recognized online? Write it down.

"It is the mark of an educated man to be able to entertain a thought without accepting it." - Aristotle

Key # 18: Show Up Online

There are over 1 billion websites online now. When my clients are just starting out, they are usually excited about finally getting their website up. They usually spend a lot of money and time designing the perfect site. Unfortunately, many waste that time and money.

I understand this desire because I was the same. It's important to realize that website developers and graphic designers are not marketing experts. They may create an aesthetically pleasing website but without good copy, no one will stay on your site.

Long gone are the days where loads of people just happen to find you online. When you're just starting, the numbers you need to create a business will not come from people that happen to come across your website, like your services and call you up to become your client.

If you have extremely good search engine optimization (SEO), you might end up on the first page of Google or Bing, but you still need to be able to engage with your potential customer. That is why chat bots on websites are so popular. People want instant gratification, instant service and instant answers. here are many apps that will simulate this experience for your visitors.

It's much different than it ever has been in the history of doing business. Social media has had a huge impact on how businesses operate. It is advisable to have a web presence online to increase your credibility, but you can also do this through other avenues.

The traditional website isn't an absolute necessity. I know gurus in the coaching industry that do not even have traditional websites and in fact, advise against them. What is necessary is to have is a form or landing page that captures names and emails.

Blogs are still popular and are a great avenue to share your content if you like to write. Many people run their business from social media and write blog-type posts there. There are many options and it really boils down to how you work best and where your customers hang out.

Contemplation

Think for a moment. How will you apply this in your business? How are you connecting and engaging with your potential customers? Do you have a way to capture names and emails? Write it down.

"We are what we repeatedly do. Excellence then, is not an act, but a habit."- Aristotle

Key # 19: Boost Your Visibility Through Consistent Profiles

Your profiles should be consistent across all your platforms. This helps to build brand recognition, credibility and visibility.

Visibility starts with your professional photos. You want people to recognize you and not have to guess if you're the same person they saw on another platform. You should have a professional photo for all your profiles and people can get to know your personality with your fun photos or "selfies".

You also want to make sure your bio is the same on LinkedIn as it is on Facebook as it is on Twitter and all social media platforms that you utilize.

You always want to make it as easy as possible for people to recognize you, know what you do, know the result you get and know who you work with. If you are communicating differently about these thing on each platform, people will get confused.

Remember, we live in the age of instant gratification. You have about 2-3 seconds to catch someone's attention. If people have to think, if they are confused, if they have to figure something out, chances are, they will not stick around.

As you are gaining clarity on your message, your audience and your solution, you want to make sure that you update your information anywhere you have a presence online.

Catch people's attention with your curiosity-provoking positioning statement. Entice people to want to find out more about you.

Consistency is key when you show up in your business both online and offline. When you connect with people virtually or in person, be consistent with your message and branding.

Contemplation

Think for a moment. How will you apply this in your business? What are all the places you have an online presence? Are your profiles all consistent? Write it down.

"Hope is the pillar that holds up the world. Hope is the dream of a waking man. "- Pliny the Elder

Key # 20: Know Where Your Audience Hangs Out Online

I remember being stumped trying to figure out where to find my audience. The problem really was that I was unclear who they even were. Once I identified them it was much easier to find where they hung out.

If you've discovered that your audience is a professional career person, then they are likely on the social media platform LinkedIn. If your audience is a younger professional, they are likely on Twitter. Many entrepreneurs and small business owners are on Instagram. This platform still largely consists of millennials. If you have a more visual brand, and your audience is a woman, you might find her on Pinterest. If your audience is a solopreneur or coach, they will likely be on Facebook. Middle-aged women and men may also be found on Facebook. There are many other social media platforms with new ones coming out every day.

You can also find your audience on popular blogs that they frequent, industry forum sites, or in different online groups. It's always good to ask during your ongoing market research where your audience hangs out.

Contemplation

Think for a moment. How will you apply this in your business? Where can you find your audience online? Write it down.

"Attitude is a little thing that makes a big difference."- Winston Churchill.

Key # 21: Be Visible as The Go-To Expert for Your Tribe

Part of having any online business includes building an audience. There are many ways to do this and I'll discuss this more in the coming keys however let's talk about the difference between an audience and a tribe.

Many entrepreneurs don't realize it, but there's a difference. Your audience includes readers, followers, and fans who are interested in your work, but may look in on the sidelines. Your tribe includes both dedicated fan and business partners or collaborators who love and adore you. They are supportive and may help you promote your offerings.

Building a tribe is the same as building a community. This means you need to give back to them. It also means being present and supportive. It requires you to be diligent at reading, commenting on, and promoting content for those people you want to join your tribe. You can even go big and tag influencers and retweet their valuable posts.

You're building a community of people who are connected, supportive, look out for one another and are engaged. To receive engagement in your community, you want to make sure you're attracting the right people, you're showing up consistently on the platforms where your audience and influencers hang out and that you're providing excellent, meaningful content.

Building a community takes dedication and time. You've got to be willing to put in your time and energy as their leader to receive engagement and connection back.

Contemplation

Think for a moment. How will you apply this in your business? How can you increase your visibility with your tribe? What can you do to build more connection and engagement within your community? Write it down.

"Know how to listen and you will profit even from those who talk badly."- Plutarch

Key # 22: Get Visible Through Email

Getting the right people on your email list is one way you can stay in front of your audience. Once you've attracted your people and you get them on your email list, you can write to them and start building a relationship with them.

Building a list of your ideal prospects allows you to stay top of mind and helps them stay engaged. People are on so many mailing lists, unsubscribes are common. Keeping them engaged with valuable information will help them decide to stay on your list.

Emailing is not dead despite what you may hear. Consistently emailing your subscribers with content that they want will increase your open rates helping you get more visible.

You are building a relationship with your subscribers. Remember that people are busy and over-stimulated. They wake up each morning to hundreds of new emails to read. You must be able to stand out.

You must be able to grab their attention. You can do that with your subject lines and by providing great information and powerful inspiration.

Find out what your audience wants to learn and give it to them in their inbox. Let them know what you're up to. Share fun tips. Be yourself and share personal stories that your audience can relate to. The key is consistently getting in front of your subscribers with relevant content that they want.

Contemplation

Think for a moment. How will you apply this in your business? How often do you email your audience? What can you do to build a better relationship with them? Write it down.

"I have often wondered how it is that every man loves himself more than all the rest of men, but yet sets less value on his own opinions of himself than on the opinions of others."- Marcus Aurelius Antonius Augustus

Key # 23: Good Copy Will Boost Your Visibility Online

You might have heard the saying before "copy is king". If you aren't writing engaging copy, you will not get new subscribers, keep old subscribers, get new customers, have an engaged tribe, or gain recognition online.

What is copy? Copy refers to the words you use when you write your content. It consists of engaging headlines, landing pages that catch your attention, the emails you send out and the blog posts and social media posts you write.

Copy includes the words on your website, in your profiles and in your bio. Copy is written words. To write good copy, you must know your dream client inside and out. One of my mentors used to say, "you've got to know what they eat for breakfast". That is how intimately you need to know them to write words that connect with them and make them stop long enough to read more. That is why headlines are so important. If headlines are written with good copy, they will make a person stop and read on.

If your words are not engaging, the person scanning what you write will not stay to read. Know your audience. Find out where they are in their journey and write in their own language. That is how you write good copy.

Contemplation

Think for a moment. How will you apply this in your business? What do you need to know about your audience to write good copy? Are you writing engaging headlines, subject lines and posts? What will make them more engaging? Write it down.

"Hope is the pillar that holds up the world. Hope is the dream of a waking man." – Gaius Plinius Secundus

Key # 24: Generate High Quality Leads

Getting traffic to your page isn't enough. You need high quality traffic to generate high quality leads. This means that you need the right kind of traffic. Getting the right kind of traffic will generate high quality leads and with good copy, your leads will convert into subscribers and some, even clients. Online business is a numbers game. You must have high numbers to make the whole online "machine" work.

There is free traffic and paid traffic. You may hear about organic traffic which refers to people who go to your site or find your page from search engines.

It's easy enough to find leads but finding the ones that will turn into prospects is another story. That is unless you are reading this book. For you, if you've gone through the keys and worked on the questions in the contemplation section, you'll be able to generate high quality leads.

Why? Because you are shining your uniqueness into the world. Because you are attracting the people who want what you have. Because you've done your homework and know where your audience hangs out. You've been giving them excellent content that they want.

You are attracting high quality leads by being you. Isn't that the best thing since sliced bread? You attract those people who you like to work with and they will like you back. You're building relationships with them and keeping them engaged within your community.

You're providing support and giving them what they want (the thing you love to do within your area of expertise). They love you for all you do. When they're ready, you can easily turn them into a client. You get to confident, visible and successful just being you!

Contemplation

Think for a moment. How will you apply this in your business? How will you attract high quality leads? What do you already have in place and what more do you need to do? Write it down.

"Say not always what you know, but always know what you say." –
Tiberius Claudius Caesar Augustus Germanicus

Key # 25: Become Visible Through Video

Video is the "it-kid" on the block and must be part of your marketing strategy! In 2017, more than 500 million hours of videos were watched on YouTube every single day. According to WordStream, an online advertising company, 45% of people watched more than an hour of Facebook videos each week and 85% of US internet audience watches videos online.

Are you using video in your marketing? If not, it's time to start. Many of my clients are very hesitant to get in front of the camera. A few concerns that my audience struggles with when starting to be on video include not looking good enough, being judged by others, not knowing what to say, sounding stupid and simply being seen

I know when I first started online, I was very uncomfortable in front of a camera. In fact, I started a radio show and was challenged a year later to do video. I knew it was time, but I wasn't ready. Then I realized, I probably would never be ready, so I jumped in.

One thing that makes video easier for me is to interview other people. That's what I've done with my Internationally Acclaimed Empowered Living Show and my Live Show, The Expert Interview Series- Online experts, instant results. My suggestion is just start. It takes practice and perseverance but in time, you will feel comfortable in front of the video camera. I'm afraid if you don't add video to your marketing strategy, you'll be left behind in the dust.

It took me a long time to switch off the professional in me and show up without make up. That was one of my biggest fears with being seen- not looking good enough. But one time after a week of extreme weather, spending my dedicated time with my animals and jumping on scheduled Facebook Live's in 110-degree heat, I had no choice but to put a bandana on my hair and show up with no trace of makeup. Under the circumstances, I surrendered because I had committed to showing up and giving excellent training to my audience.

I've realized that people don't really care so much what you look like, but rather the powerful way in which you show up and give value.

Contemplation

Think for a moment. How will you apply this in your business? If you are not doing video, what is stopping you? If you are doing video, what can you do enhance your practice? Write it down.

"If you have overcome your inclination and not been overcome by it, you have reason to rejoice."- Titus Maccius Plautus

Key # 26: Tell Engaging Stories

Most cultures use storytelling to pass down culture, history and legends. People have gathered together to share stories since the dawn of man. Although the tradition and rituals of storytelling is mostly gone, it still has its place especially in your business.

Client testimonials and case studies tell the story of how you can get your clients results. These stories create an emotional bond with the reader. Even masters at sales use storytelling to get their point across and bond with their listener by sharing examples in place of facts and stats. Building engagement is nearly effortless when you use storytelling.

According to Forbes contributor Billee Howard, storytelling is the "new strategic imperative of business" where we can use emotional along with rational engagement integrating both the mind and heart of your listener.

It's important to be able to bring dry facts to life through a real-life experience in a story. People are attracted to stories because people are social beings.

Most stories have an arch to them such as in a "hero's journey" where the hero of the story goes on some adventure, overcomes an obstacle and wins a victory that transforms his life. These kinds of stories are popular formulas in video sales pages, webinars and speeches.

Storytelling should be part of every brand. This is one skill that I'll always be working on. I know how important it is in helping your brand become recognizable and therefore, more visible online.

Contemplation

Think for a moment. How will you apply this in your business? What stories can you think of that will help your audience realize the results you are able to achieve with your clients? What story can you tell to create brand recognition? Write it down.

"Continuous effort - not strength or intelligence - is the key to unlocking our potential."- Winston Churchill

Key # 27: Get Visible with Speaking

There are many ways to get visible through speaking both online and offline. Speaking is a way to share your story and experiences with the audience and build a relationship along with the know, like and trust factor. Telling your story helps you showcase your journey as well as to your expertise.

Online you can create webinars, interviewed on podcasts, radio shows and summits. It's easy to create a webinar that educates, entertains and inspires your audience.

The more engaging your presentation or interview, the more your audience will remember you. There are also specific formulas that help to create curiosity, engagement and enticement to bring forth more sales for the person your offer is the right fit for.

Having your own podcast, radio show or video show is another way to showcase your expertise. I love to interview others because I get to learn about my guest's expertise, showcase them in front of my audience and at the same time, highlight my expertise.

Speaking offline in your community is another strategy to become more visible. Both online and offline strategies are necessary to boost visibility and brand recognition. If you're not currently speaking on stage, doing workshops locally or speaking at local meet-ups, this is something to strive for. Toastmasters International is a great way to get more comfortable speaking.

Contemplation

Think for a moment. How will you apply this in your business? Where can you speak online and offline? What topics will help showcase your expertise? Write it down.

"Everything flows and nothing abides, everything gives way and nothing stays fixed.". - Heraclitus

Key # 28: Write a Book to Boost Visibility

Writing a book is one way to showcase your expertise and help your audience discover your philosophy and personality. Some people say that writing a book is like having a business card on steroids.

This is my third book. I started as a co-author of the book "Supercharge Your Success" which became a Bestseller and co-authored "My Big Idea" which became an International Bestseller. There are many opportunities to co-author books or be in a compilation-type book with others.

The beauty of having a book, either one that you authored on your own or that you co-authored, is that you are seen as an expert in your area. Writing a book has many advantages for your online business.

Although you won't likely get rich selling your books, they help your credibility and can supplement your following's learning.

There are other options to become an author. You can write an ebook which usually is a downloadable book to offer your subscribers. You can write a digital book such as a Kindle.

Today, you are fortunate that there are so many options available. No longer do you have to go through a pricey publicist unless you choose to go that route. You can easily self-publish your own ebook, digital book or paperback book (like this one).

Contemplation

Think for a moment. How will you apply this in your business? What kind of book will you write to showcase your expertise, philosophy and personality? Write it down.

"Time is the wisest counselor of all."- Pericles

Key # 29: Be Visible on Social Media

I've written briefly about social media throughout this book. Social media is here to stay. It's a part of doing business online. You will not be visible if you are not part of the social media revolution.

Earlier, I suggested where to find your audience on social media. When you find out where your audience hangs out, you want to be visible on that platform.

Social media is important as it highlights not only your expertise, but a behind-the-scenes view of your brand personality. Engagement on social media is one your company's biggest assets. Likes, shares, comments all increase your visibility not only to your audience, but to new audiences that may contain your ideal client. To earn likes, shares and comments, you must be producing high quality content.

Remember that in the beginning, your business is built one person at a time and it's often necessary to put in some manual work reaching out to those who you think would be a good fit for your services.

You can start with your social media profile. This is the first thing people see when they want to consider your brand. Use keywords in your company profile description. Doing this, will increase your visibility in search engines and depending on the algorithm of the platform, could instantly increase your visibility to potential followers.

Another consideration is the time of day and day of the week that you post. You can look at your insights on social media to see when your followers are present. Using hashtags can also boost the reach of your post. Hashtags are used on most social media platforms. People use hashtags to search for content. If you use popular hashtags, and use them the right way, you can get your content in front of your ideal audience.

One of the best ways to gain visibility on social media is to leverage those who already have achieved influencer status. Always start a relationship by giving. Social media marketing is a popular online strategy because it is cost-effective, versatile and builds over time.

Contemplation

Think for a moment. How will you apply this in your business? Are your profiles optimized on all your platforms? Write it down.

"True wisdom comes to each of us when we realize how little we understand about life, ourselves, and the world around us."- Socrates

Key # 30: Build A Tribe Container

Now that you know who your audience is, what social media platform they hang out on, and what solution they want, you can start to create a container for your audience. I call this a "tribe incubator".

A tribe incubator is a place where you nurture and grow your audience. Think of this as a group on social media. If your audience is on LinkedIn, you want to start your own LinkedIn group. If your audience is on Instagram, you can start an Instagram Pod, if your audience is on Facebook then you want to start a Facebook group and so on. The beauty of a tribe incubator is that you can get in front of your audience any time you want.

When you run the group, you are the leader and you will need to have rules to abide by. You get to showcase your leadership and facilitator abilities. As the leader of your tribe incubator, you create the culture you want. I like to create a nurturing, inspiring group that offers excellent content on both strategy and mindset. Most people get stuck behind fears and beliefs so helping people overcome those obstacles helps them move forward. But just because the environment is nurturing, and inspiring doesn't mean that I can't gently call someone out on what is keeping them stuck. I do this because it does no good to enable people who are trying to get unstuck.

In your incubator you can do what you want. One of the best parts of being the leader of your group and having an incubator is that you have built your own type of focus group. One that is a slice of your audience who can represent your whole audience. You can ask market research questions. You give excellent content and support to your people, and they will give back to you when you ask them questions. It's a win-win!

Contemplation

Think for a moment. How will you apply this in your business? Do you have a tribe container? What platform will you lead your tribe? What kind of culture do you want in your group? Write it down.

"The way to gain a good reputation is to endeavor to be what you desire to appear."- Socrates

Key # 31: Automate to Be Visible Everywhere

If you want to be visible everywhere, you need some help. You can't do it all on your own. You can either hire a Virtual Assistant to help you or you can use automation software.

Right now, as I write this book, I've seen a trend on social media platforms. Third-party applications have been used for years but now they are starting to either prohibit their use, make them difficult to use, or punish you for their use.

Different platforms have different guidelines and it's important to be aware of them as well as being aware of industry trends. For instance, one social media platform just announced that they will be basically punishing pages or groups that do not have engagement. Therefore, using a third-party post publisher will not help you if people are not engaging with the post. When you have poor engagement (lack of comments, likes, follows), you will be "punished" and the platform will not show your posts to your audience.

If you have a large group or many people in your contacts, if they aren't engaging, it may be time to clean house. On the other hand, using your favorite platform's internal automation is favored. Bots are becoming extremely popular and you will likely see more robotics online.

Humans and digital workforces create unstoppable momentum in your business. Bots are considered part of your marketing team. Selecting the right technology, the right platform and the right digital application is necessary.

As an entrepreneur, you wear many hats. The great thing is, you don't have to do all this alone. There's always automation!

Contemplation

Think for a moment. How will you apply this in your business? What is your favorite platform's internal application? How can you build engagement using a virtual or digital team? Write it down.

"Make the best use of what's in your power and take the rest as it happens."- Epictetus

Key # 32: Attracting Visibility Through Authenticity

Attracting visibility doesn't mean acting crazy to stand out online. But it does mean expressing your viewpoints, showcasing your expertise and getting in front of the right audience.

When you've gained clarity, confidence and you know who your audience is, all topics that have been covered in the first part of this book, you'll be ready to attract visibility through your authentic voice. You will be ready to be seen and be ready to start expressing yourself.

Authenticity is a buzz word and it's overused. However, it does get the point across. I used to struggle with what it really meant to be authentic (because I was a perfectionist, I wanted to be authentic the "right" way).

What I've realized is that being authentic isn't' something you have to think about. It's not some deep secret from your past. Being authentic is being who you are RIGHT NOW. You are creating your future this very moment. You can choose to be whomever you want in this very moment. Who are you choosing to be?

When you think about authenticity in this manner, it has a different spin. Because you choose who you want in any moment and show up that way. Who do you want to be? How do you want to show up? How do you want to be seen? These are all great questions to ask yourself.

When you show up powerfully, confidently and command attention, you will receive it. When you are showing up in front of your people as their go-to expert, in the incubator you've created, and you are giving them what they want to learn, you will have the visibility you're looking for.

You will become more confident with your online presence. You will attract more of the people who are your ideal audience simply by being authentic- choosing to be who you want to be in the moment.

Contemplation

Think for a moment. How will you apply this in your business? How are you choosing to show up? How do you want to be seen? What do you need to do to bridge the gap? Write it down.

"Wisdom begins wonder." – Socrates

Key # 33: Unleash Your Mojo Online

This is my group brand command. It's time for you to have a good understanding of what it means. You have read this far, it is now time for you to unleash your mojo- your essence, your energy online.

Unleashing your mojo online means that you show up as the powerful person that you are, expressing yourself verbally, visually and energetically in front of people that want what you have to offer. Be bold. Be courageous. It's time for you to step up and become the person you want to be. It's time to show your audience who their real leader is- unabashedly and unapologetically.

It took me some time to become myself online. First, I had to find "me" again. I had to figure out how I wanted to show up, who I wanted to be and how I wanted to be seen. Like I have said over again, it's a journey. It is a process. The exploration and expansion will never end.

Being able to unleash your mojo online usually doesn't happen overnight. Think of a caterpillar. The caterpillar lives its short life. For the caterpillar to turn into the beautiful butterfly, it must digest itself, marinating in the unknown, being present and surrendering. Then a metamorphosis can occur.

Now see yourself going through this process as an entrepreneur online. Imagine the caterpillar, cocoon and butterfly stages. When you're able to let go of the past, focus on being present and allow your journey to take you to places you can't yet imagine, then you know you're ready to fly like a butterfly. You're ready to share your energy with the world. You're ready to unleash your mojo online!

Contemplation

Think for a moment. How will you apply this in your business? In what stage of metamorphosis are you? What does it mean to you to unleash your mojo online? Who do you need to become to be the person that you want to show up as? Write it down.

"Do not dwell in the past, do not dream of the future, concentrate the mind on the present moment." -Buddha

Success
Get ready to soar beyond your imagination!

Key # 34: Your Audience's Journey

Up to this point, we've covered how to gain confidence by discovering your message, identify who your audience is and where they hang out. You've realized that you must show up as who you want to become to energetically attract people and become visible.

You've done the deep inner work by writing out the answers to the questions in the contemplation section. Now, you're ready for success! Now, you're ready to put the puzzle pieces together to get noticed and get clients online.

You won't find many experts who explain the audience journey and I find that it brings so much clarity when you understand this piece. Your audience will range from people who are stuck to those who are ready to get results. Think of it like a timeline. Those people at point A are stuck and sitting on the sidelines watching you. They are stuck, so they are not ready to take action. They don't even know what they want or need at this point. They will still be part of your audience, but they will not be your dream client.

Your dream client is on the other end of the timeline towards point Z. They are the ones who are ready and actively seeking a solution to their problem. They have tried one or many things before to get them unstuck but nothing has worked to get them results so far. That's where you come in.

Now there are people in your audience all along the timeline from point A to point Z. At each point they will have slightly different characteristics because they are at a different point in their journey from being stuck to being ready to get a result. Knowing your audience and where they are on their journey will help you identify your dream clients.

You will still be educating, nurturing and adding value to everyone in your audience from point A to point Z. Always talk to those in your audience the way you would talk to your dream client. This helps to pull the stuck people up, lifting them and inspiring them to someday be ready to take action.

Contemplation

Think for a moment. How will you apply this in your business? What is your audience's journey? What are the characteristics of those who are at point A? What are the characteristics of those who are your dream clients ready to work with you? Write it down.

"We are shaped by our thoughts; we become what we think. When the mind is pure, joy follows like a shadow that never leaves."- Buddha

Key # 35: Create Hot Offers

There are certain characteristics of a hot offer. You want to be able to craft these offers so that your audience wants what you have. You want to make your offers easy to say either no or yes to.

The first thing to start with is your free gift. This is something that you give to your new subscriber where they can get to know you and you start to build a relationship with them. You must build a connection with them before they'll be ready to say yes to your paid offer. Your free content must provide actual value so that your new subscriber will get a small win or result.

Creating hot offers starts with your market research. When you've done this correctly, you will get the words (copy) to put on your landing page or sales page. These words that you use will help them connect, engage and say to themselves- yes, she gets me.

It's always helpful to have social proof or testimonials on your page. This helps potential subscribers see the value in your offer. Many marketing experts suggest you have a front-end offer that is a low-cost offer. This is because the more times your people say yes to something, whether it's replying to an email, giving you feedback in a survey, clicking on a link or opt-in into a free gift, the more likely they are to spend money with you.

Hot offers are irresistible to your dream client. They paint a picture of the outcomes they will get when they receive your product or service. When creating a hot offer for a paid program or package, there are a few components that must be in place. You must have what your prospect wants. It must be packaged in a way that they understand the results or outcomes they will achieve. Create a sense of urgency to get people to take action (remember, learning information and not applying is what keeps people stuck and you want to move them forward to a decision). And it's important to show the value and savings as well as offering bonuses.

Contemplation

Think for a moment. How will you apply this in your business? What types of offers do you have? Do you have all the necessary components? If not, what do you need to revise? Write it down.

"You, yourself, as much as anybody in the entire universe, deserve your love and affection."- Buddha

.

Key # 36: Create Profitable Programs

I've already written about building your tribe incubator or container to house your audience. When you're creating a program, you want to make sure the content is geared to get a tangible result.

Most people are tired of taking self-study courses that are long and arduous and don't get results. The reason self-study programs yield poor results no matter how good the content, is because there is no accountability. Remember, people love to learn but they find it difficult to implement what they learn.

I can't tell you how many of my new clients tell me they want to create a membership site and make a lot of money. They have great ideas about all the content they will provide and how many people will buy into it. The problem is that membership sites are going the way of the dodo bird. Sure, they'll still be in existence and they can still be useful if done correctly. However, when someone is left to their own devices, unfortunately old habits and patterns sneak in and membership sites lose engagement, or the self-study course ends up taking up space on their computer instead of showing up as a result in their business.

That is why most of my courses have a component of live support from me personally. People want interaction. They want to know they will get their individual questions answered. They want to know they'll be supported. They like structure and they want to get results.

Profitable programs are created with the priority on getting results. Make it easy for your customers to say yes to your program. Set up payment plans. Provide additional support. Give them something no one else is offering.

Exude your one-of-a-kindness. Excellent customer service and support is non-negotiable. Profitable programs are created by people going through your program and referring it to other's because they had such a great experience and amazing results.

Contemplation

Think for a moment. How will you apply this in your business? What do you need to do to create a profitable program? Write it down.

"Pleasure in the job puts perfection in the work."- Aristotle

Key # 37: You Must Sell to Make Money

To be successful, you must generate income in your business. I came from a background in health and wellness. I never had to promote myself. I worked behind the scenes. Unless you have a sales, marketing or advertising background, you are likely not sales savvy. You might even cringe at the word sales. I did, and I know my clients do when they first start working with me.

However, if you want to be in business, you've got to be able to sell your goods. Selling doesn't have to be hard, sleazy, pushy or conniving. You don't have to convince people to buy your products and services if you are using the keys I've written about previously. You understand that your clients are on a journey and each one will be somewhere from point A to point Z. You understand that those people in your audience toward point Z are ready to get a result. This means that they are willing to pay you to finally get a result if they believe you are the one that can help them.

If you've been following along and giving excellent content, showing social proof and exuding your mojo, your potential clients will adore you, trust you and be willing to give you their hard-earned money for your solution.

When I first started online, I thought it would be easier if I learned how to sell through a sales page or through email. But I struggled to make money. I avoided getting on the phone with someone and having an actual sales conversation at all costs. But this is where you must start.

Each time you get on the phone with a prospective client, you understand them better. You start to see a trend of their problems; their desires and you begin to understand how you can best help them. Don't shy away from getting on a call and having an enrollment or sales conversation.

This is how you start to generate income for your coaching business. Believe me, eventually, you'll have a blast with sales! Always be of service. Creating an impact is not about making money. Making money is part of what happens when you make an impact.

Contemplation

Think for a moment. How will you apply this in your business? How are you generating income? Are you having sales conversations? If not, what is stopping you? Write it down.

"Do not consider painful what is good for you."-Euripides

Key # 38: Create Processes & Systems

Part of having a successful business is having rinse and repeat processes and systems that you can implement so you don't have to recreate the wheel. These are often called Standard Operating Procedures or SOPs.

Identify what types of actions that you engage in daily which help you reach your goals. Write a process or method of operation for each of these actions. Each time you do something new, make sure you have a process or system. If you don't have one, it's time to create one.

Creating systems and processes will not only help you when you first get started, but it will help you when you decide to delegate tasks. Eventually you will get to the point when you no longer want to spend time on tasks that are not in y our area of expertise. This is when it's time to delegate.

When you have SOPs, it helps you get work done in an organized way. Creating SOPs for your marketing strategy will allow you to have an increased return on investment for your marketing efforts.

Here are three areas to start creating your SOPs: Marketing, Workflow and Bookkeeping.

It's important to review these on a routine basis or when you're having areas that are not working as efficiently as you'd like.

When I worked in Corporate America, streamlining processes was one of my skills and I have been able to bring my expertise to my business.

I am confident that you have skills in your tool bag that will help you in creating systems and processes. The best part about having your own business is that you get to set up systems and processes that work best for you!

Contemplation

Think for a moment. How will you apply this in your business? What processes or systems do you have in place? What SOPs do you need to create so you are ready to delegate? Write it down.

"Not even the gods fight against necessity."- Simonides

Key # 39: Build Your Email List

Any successful entrepreneur that has a business online will tell you that their success is largely due to their email list and that the amount of success parallels the size of their email list. If you don't have an email list, you want to start now.

You may be wondering how you get people onto your email list and grow the size. There are many ways to do this. You'll need a form where people can enter their name and email. You'll need an email service provider. There are many that are free with a limit on the number of subscribers and there are some that have free trials. I recommend that you try a few out and see which feels easiest to navigate.

I wrote about free offers that give excellent value and give your subscriber a small result or win previously. You can promote these free offers out on social media, or on your website. You will need to drive traffic (people) to your offer to get them to sign up.

You can also write a blog post and insert a supplemental learning guide that they must opt in for. You can add a link to your free gift in your general email signature area. You can do live videos and direct your audience to subscribe to get the offer.

When you're offering a training, you can have people sign up. When you are being interviewed, you are often invited to share your free offer. You can go into groups and promote your offer if the administrator allows this. You can put your link in your author box when you submit articles for marketing. You can ask people to share your offer if they found it useful and you can reach out to people who might be a good fit for your community and invite them to download your offer.

These are all ways to build your email list. Remember that you don't just want anyone on your list. You want YOUR people. Your ideal audience that you can connect with and who will engage.

Eventually when your list grows to at least 5000 people, you will be invited to speak on more summits and you will be able to rub arms with other experts and influencers that to increase your visibility and success.

Contemplation

Think for a moment. How will you apply this in your business? What can new strategies can you add to build your list? Write it down.

"Pleasure in the job puts perfection in the work"- Aristotle.

Key # 40: Funnels 101

You've probably heard people in the online industry talk about funnels. What the heck are they and how do you use them are the questions I usually get.

I remember learning about funnels back in 2010 when people first started talking about them in the internet marketing industry. They've really taken off since then, but they are not new. Creating a funnel is just a new way of looking at your sales process.

The top of the funnel which is the widest, represents the largest number of your audience. These will be all the people from point A to point Z I've written about in previous keys. As the funnel narrows, there will be less and less people. The people that are at the narrowest end of the funnel are your high-paying clients.

You can easily create a simple funnel online. It starts with your landing page. This is where you will ask your audience to subscribe or opt-in to your email list. The next step is considered a front-end offer. This would be an offer for something that your audience wants at a low price which makes it an easy decision for them to say yes. If your audience purchases this offer, the next step is to create an upsell offer. This would be an offer for a product or service that would help them benefit from the first offer only at a higher price.

Think McDonalds "would you like a shake with that" might be the first offer and then when they say yes, they might get another offer such as "would you like to try our special" which might be a higher price. I personally haven't been to McDonalds in years so this may be an outdated example, but you get the idea. If they did not go for the special in this example, then the next part in the funnel might be an offer that is lower than the special but costs more than just ordering the shake. This helps to know exactly what your audience wants so you can continue to give them more of the same in your free content and paid offers.

A funnel is simply the steps that a lead goes through your process to become a paying customer.

Contemplation

Think for a moment. How will you apply this in your business? What does your online funnel look like? How do you get most of the people in the top section and what do you offer those at the bottom of the funnel? Write it down.

"Always give – even if all you have is a little bit."- Buddha

Key # 41: Collaboration Creates Success

Even though you are an entrepreneur and in business by yourself does not mean you can build your business and become successful by yourself.

You must be able to work with others in your community and be able to collaborate with people that can help you grow your business.

Collaboration is essential to your success. There is power in numbers. You may have heard the term Referral Partners or JV partners (joint venture partners) before. These are collaborators. Your partners who will have the same audience as you do but offer complimentary services will add value to your audience and vice versa.

Think of a relationship coach for women who partners with a health coach for women. You can see there is mutual value that can be offered the same audience.

When you're well-connected online, you will be more approachable and visible for potential collaborations. Collaborations could include doing webinars for each other's audiences. It's also common to promote their product to your audience when what they offer is not in your area of expertise but would add value to your people.

Partnering with people will get your name out into the industry community. Don't be afraid to reach out to potential partners and industry influencers. You have something unique to bring to the table that no one else does. Don't ever forget that!

Contemplation

Think for a moment. How will you apply this in your business? Think about your expertise and your audience. What type of service would be complimentary? Who can you identify within your connections that you are willing to reach out to and discuss a potential collaboration? Write it down.

"Unity can only be manifested by the Binary. Unity itself and the idea of Unity are already two."- Buddha

Key # 42: Self-Care is Essential for Your Success

It's very easy to get wrapped up in your day-to-day activities as a business owner. When you have your own business, the work is never done.

I see many driven women that come from high-stress careers go into coaching to help others. They bring their corporate habits to their business that caused burn-out in the first place. They feel a need to go, go, go and then end up exhausted, frazzled and wondering if this business is really the right thing to do. If this sounds like you, you're not alone. This is common.

It's essential to weave self-care into your daily routine. This includes the right nourishment, good amounts of sleep, turning off your electronics, setting boundaries around the times you work, allowing time for family, a social life, inspiration and relaxation.

When you start to see momentum occur in your business, it's easy to want to continue to work. Often slowing down helps you speed up. Nourish your body with whole, clean foods that energize you. Exercise, stretch, go for a walk or do yoga to release stress and keep the oxygen flowing. Have a wake-up time and bed time routine. Avoid sitting at your computer all day long. Instead, take short breaks throughout the day. I get focused and want to keep working so I set notifications to remind me when to get on my elliptical or go outside for fresh air.

When you don't give yourself time for self-care, you will burn out. I believe this is one reason why many people end up quitting or simply fail in their business.

Be aware of your energy because how you feel affects how you show up in the world. Your energy, attitudes and beliefs affect what kind of content you create, how your potential clients see you and how you can be unconsciously repelling clients.

Take time for yourself for pampering. You work hard, and you deserve it! Allow yourself to celebrate your victories!

Contemplation

Think for a moment. How will you apply this in your business? What kind of self-care routines have you set up? What do you need to do to take better care of yourself? Write it down.

"Health is the greatest gift, contentment the greatest wealth, faithfulness the best relationship."- Buddha

Key # 43: Feeling Unworthy Impacts Your Business

Questioning your worthiness is very typical as you're growing your business. The "Worthiness" energy drain is often so silent that you aren't even aware that you have it. It preys on your feelings leaching your energy as you go about your day leaving you feeling beat up, dragged through the ringer or wanting to run and hide- which will not help your business, am I right?

Entrepreneurs with this type of energy drain are often in the service business and tend to be highly sensitive. They love to help others. The problem is that they don't ever have time for themselves. They feel resentful of their situation, guilty when they slow down to rest and they like to numb out to escape reality.

The Worthiness energy drain is associated with the emotional baggage you carry around from childhood. The patterns were created at that point in time when you first learned how to cope with certain hurtful, traumatic, scary, or devastating situations.

These coping skills protected you throughout the years. But when you started to outgrow them (and didn't know how to replace them with a healthier set of coping skills) they began to cause continuous energy leaks.

Outgrowing old patterns or beliefs that have been handed down to you from authority figures can make you feel uncomfortable, boxed in, or trapped.

These patterns create the need to seek the approval of others to validate your thoughts, beliefs, and feelings. This habit of seeking answers and validation outside of yourself contributes to the Worthiness energy drain.

As your energy becomes depleted, it makes you feel more self-conscious and affects your self-esteem. You can see how this can affect your business. You may find it difficult to charge high enough prices that match your value. You may be giving sessions away for free because you want to help when in fact you are doing them a disservice.

When you are not able to stand up for yourself, then you can't possibly hold your clients to their highest self. This shows up as a sluggish business with a lack of momentum.

People who have suffer from the Worthiness energy drain fear vulnerability and visibility. This is one area that I work on with my clients who have tried to get "out there" online and find no one is noticing them. We delve into this energy drain because it has to be cleared to allow visibility.

Emotions that are not released but rather "stuffed" take up space in your body. The Worthiness energy drain can accumulate inside you, manifesting as a real blockage in your body. You may experience this as a health condition, feeling stuck in your business or trapped in your life.

The Worthiness energy drain constantly depletes your energy as you give your power away to people and situations. Because you don't like conflict you will find situations where you're not able to stand up for yourself very tiring even when you're not physically tired.

One important thing to know is that situations that seem to trigger this worthiness drain are simply arising to show you repeatedly that what you need to be aware of. When you don't address the feelings, you will feel exhausted and perhaps, empty. Next time you notice this cycle ask yourself why this is happening again. Pay attention to the pattern and notice what it is trying to teach you.

One quick solution is to become aware of your feelings and emotions giving them names. Taking this action is a way of acknowledging the emotion. Here is an exercise to help you shift the emotion:

Feel the emotion inside of you. Where is it? What does it feel like? What is it trying to tell you? Ask it- and be receptive to the answer. Now match what you are feeling inside your body with an expression, a movement or a noise (for example, growling when you feel trapped and you're your stomach is burning). Then, thank the emotion for being there to protect you. Lastly, with gratitude, send it off into the ether.

Contemplation

Think for a moment. How will you apply this in your business and life? Do you suffer from the Worthiness energy drain? How is it showing up in your business? Write it down.

"We are shaped by our thoughts; we become what we think. When the mind is pure, joy follows like a shadow that never leaves."- Buddha

Key # 44: How the Judgement Energy Drain Affects Your Business

The "Judgement" energy drain occurs within the never-ending thoughts that spin in your head. It sucks your power or energy by keeping you up at night worrying excessively about things. You may find yourself thinking about the same thing that happened in the past repeatedly and unable to get it out of your head. People with this kind of drain use the words "should" or "could" or "would have" often.

This drain creates fear about your situation and can make you think that instead of living a great life, you're barely getting by or simply surviving. It uses up your energy on thoughts that you think are important and urgent when if you were able to take a step back, you'd see that they are inconsequential or petty. This drain impacts your business by keeping you stuck and playing small.

When you have the judgement energy drain, you feel tired and overwhelmed by the tasks you should do. Your energy is drained from being judgmental of yourself or others. If you have this drain, your self-talk is worse than the way you'd talk to your worst enemy. You like control but doubt yourself and unconsciously close off opportunities that could expand your business and make you feel more fulfilled. You're a perfectionist.

You may sleep out of boredom or frustration- not necessarily because you're physically tired but because you need to stop the thought spiral in your head. You may try to plug up this energy drain by avoiding situations, trying to control others or the expected outcome of a situation.

This drain is caused by living in the past or the future, from information overload, or an overstimulating environment where you feel the need to be "on" all the time. It could also be caused by too much clutter which blocks your thought flow, or from not having enough personal time to decompress.

You can see how this affects your business mojo. The main solution to this judgement energy drain is to live in the present moment. To be present, you must be able to quiet your mind.

Take time to quiet your mind. This may sound like an easy solution but if you have this type of energy drain, quieting your mind will be challenging.

One of the easiest ways to quiet your mind is to go outside in nature and instead of focusing on the thoughts in our head, close your eyes and listen to the pleasant sounds around you.

You can also get involved with a charity or volunteer somewhere where there are people that are less fortunate than you. The point here is to take your focus off your thoughts spinning in your head.

Contemplation

Think for a moment. How will you apply this in your life and business? Do you suffer from the Judgement energy drain? How is affecting your business? What can you do to dissolve it? Write it down.

"No one saves us but ourselves. No one can and no one may. We ourselves must walk the path."- Buddha

Key # 45: The Most Dangerous Energy Drain

The "Disconnection" drain is closely tied to your business mojo because it affects how you show up in the world.

This drain sucks the joy and playfulness out of your life. If you find yourself to be very serious, focused on time or you're militant about structure, you likely have this type of energy drain. If you're a workaholic, feel like life's too hard or you have bad luck, you smile infrequently and don't do anything for fun routinely, you are probably affected by this energy drain.

This is the most dangerous of the energy drains. It's dangerous because you fill yourself up with the belief that you must become something more than you already are; and that you aren't already successful. This drain makes you feel disconnected from your essence, your mojo and from everyone and everything.

Here are some symptoms of the disconnection energy drain: This drain smashes your self-worth, keeps you feeling unsuccessful and feeling shameful or guilty. Without trying to, you repel people. When you're out of alignment, energetically people feel confused and in business, they'll pass you over and move to the next business. This drain makes you feel separated from everyone and everything around you. You may even feel invisible or unheard. Your life can feel miserable, as if you're trapped or a prisoner of your own life.

This energy drain is caused by being out of alignment with who you really are. It's important to align yourself with who you are BECOMING, and what you want out of life. You get out of alignment when you don't trust your gut feelings and when you look for validation from outside sources.

You forget that you already have within you everything you've always wanted and needed. You already ARE enough. Just by being here right now, being you- you are enough. You don't have to be anything more than who you are.

You were born with everything in you already. Your challenge is to figure out who you are, what you came here for, what message you are here to bring to others, and how to enjoy life being YOU and all the goodness you bring to the world.

Although this is the most dangerous types of energy drain, it's the simplest to fix. Once you suspect you have this type of energy drain, the fastest way to eliminate it is to give up control of what is.

If you have this type of energy drain, giving up control is going to be difficult because the disconnection energy drain affects your identity. Your ego wants control. Giving up control or accepting what is, involves trust and faith and that's the only way that you can stop this drain.

Fixing this drain involves developing trust and a deep knowing that life is happening FOR you and not TO you. Which can be very challenging when your business isn't getting the results you want.

Contemplation

Think for a moment. How will you apply this in your life and business? Do you suffer from the disconnection energy drain? How does it affect you in your business? What are you going to do to fix this drain? Write it down.

"When your mind is free of desires, it's also free of the prison we call fear."- Buddha

Key # 46: Become Unstoppable

To be unstoppable, you've got to release emotional blockages that are keeping you in fear, holding you back and keeping you from being where you want to be in your life, or who you are here to become.

Get rid of lifestyle habits that create distractions for you and your business. Start living in the present moment without perseverating on the past or expecting specific outcomes for the future. The present is NOW. Anything is possible when you live in the MOMENT.

Connect to your internal wisdom- look inside for answers instead of looking outside yourself.

How you show up energetically will either attract or repel your audience. They feel when you're not in alignment, when you're not congruent or in integrity with your own self. Showing up in alignment, as the best, most empowered version of yourself is what will unleash your mojo. And, it's a process. It's a journey so don't be hard on yourself.

Being 100% congruent and in alignment with everything you do is the only way to be in flow and it's the key to abundance, prosperity and effortlessness. When you achieve this, you finally feel like you are supported- in your business, by your clients, with your family and in life.

Contemplation

Think for a moment. How will you apply this in your business? What is preventing you from being unstoppable? What can you do to overcome this? Write it down.

"You can't travel the path until you become the path."- Buddha

Key # 47: Shifting into Flow

Imagine what it would be like if you were living the exact life you desired? Imagine doing what you loved every single day and being paid for what you do best- being you. This is what happens when you shift into flow.

When you're in flow, life and business are effortless instead of effortful. So often people are stuck in the hardships of life. It doesn't have to be that way. You can create life by design. It's within your power.

I believe that you begin to create momentum by making decisions. You can create from the thoughts you have but you don't set things in motion until you make a conscious decision to act upon that thought.

Have you ever wanted to work with a coach, go to an event or travel somewhere but you didn't have the money? You try and try but cannot figure out a way. You may want to go so badly, you pray, meditate or wish for it to happen. You may ask the Universe to deliver it to you. But until you decide, the deed is not a done deal.

What do you want in your life? How do you want your business to operate? What is a perfect day for you? How would you create a life by design?

I've written in the beginning of the book how following joy can help you navigate life. Follow your joy. What do you love to do? Do more of it! What do you want your life to be like? Make it more like that. Who do you want to become? Start becoming that person. This is how you shift into flow. This is when things become effortless. This is when synchronicities and miracles occur every single day of your life! Have fun. Take time to smell the roses. Go out in nature and soak up the sunshine. Do what makes you happy and see how your life changes.

Contemplation

Think for a moment. How will you apply this in your business? What do you need to do to shift into flow in your life? Contemplate some of the question I asked in this key. Write the answers down.

"You can only find peace within. Do not seek peace without."- Buddha

Key # 48: Achieving Success

What is your definition of success? If you think about it, achieving success is not reaching a goal. Success is the feeling you get when you achieve a goal or a dream.

Think about how you want to feel when you reach your goals. Hold on to that feeling. Keep that feeling alive inside you day in and day out. That is the energy that is attractive. That is the mojo that becomes reality.

You are already successful. You already have everything within you right now. What needs to shift for you to feel successful? What is the feeling that is missing?

It's important to be organized in your day so that you can be more productive. Block out times for certain tasks in your business. Try not to multi-task. This is one habit that I've had to curtail. I used to have a handful of projects I was working on at any given time. Now, I set time aside to work on one at a time. Set certain times to create and send out your emails. Make time for potential client connections. Schedule times you are available for sales calls.

Have specific blocks of time set for creating content. If you don't schedule times for different tasks, you will feel scattered. It's difficult to track your progress when you aren't organized. One action that has helped me is to write down my "wins" or results at the end of each day. As a business owner, you are so busy and wear so many different hats, if you don't keep track of what you've accomplished it can feel like you're never getting ahead. Take time out each night to write out what you've done so you can look back and see all the progress you've made.

Contemplation

Think for a moment. How will you apply this in your business? What is your definition of success? What feeling does it give you? What activities will make you feel more productive and successful? Write it down.

"Each morning we are born again. It is what we do today that matters most."- Buddha

Key # 49: Your Strategic Plan

Aligning everything to your vision is the key when creating a strategic plan.

What goals do you want to accomplish each quarter? What actions must you do to accomplish each goal? You want to be able to measure your success by tracking your numbers.

What is your marketing strategy? What details will help you bring that strategy to life? You want your plan to be simple and achievable. The goals should all align to reach your vision.

You can include customer feedback and SWOT analysis (strengths, weaknesses, opportunities and threats). The simple point is to break down your big goals that will help you reach your vision into smaller, actionable steps that you can then break down into daily tasks.

Be consistent. Consistency is the key in growing your business. It may not feel like you're gaining traction but stick with it and you'll see that consistency does make a difference.

Contemplation

Think for a moment. How will you apply this in your business? What goals will help you reach your vision? How can you break those down into smaller steps and daily tasks to write your strategic plan? Write it down.

"The root of all suffering is the attachment."- Buddha

Key # 50: Soar Beyond Imagination!

You've reached the final key and you are ready to soar! How you view life will impact the success of your business. How you view yourself will impact your productivity and therefore success. Be open to different perspectives.

Success isn't all about numbers or reaching the finish line. It's a process. Enjoy the process. Use all your senses to be present each day. Be open to miracles and synchronicities. The more you notice them, the more they will occur. Remember, the magic is in the unknown.

You don't have to be in control of everything in your life. Sometimes, you need to let go, surrender and just allow. Sometimes you must slow down, to speed up. Practice unattachment. This has been a huge lesson for me. What I found out is that the only place true freedom really exists when you are not attached. This includes attachment to old, outdated material things, old habits that don't serve you anymore, patterns from the distant past that you continue to carry around keeping you stuck and attachment to outcomes.

Be unattached. This doesn't mean that you don't care or that you don't set goals. But it gives you space to allow flow. And when you shift into flow, you are in the place of the unknown. This is a powerful place to be. You are not in control of the outcome. You've released attachment and can enjoy each moment.

I realized when I was meditating on my favorite rock in my horse pasture one day, that in each moment, there is never anything wrong. When you're able to be present to right now, there is only bliss.

When you live moment to moment, your business will take off and you will personally soar- beyond your imagination! The magic begins when you are ready to claim your brilliance!

Contemplation

Think for a moment. How will you apply this in your business? What are you attached to that you are willing be free of? Are you ready to claim your brilliance? Write it down.

"Doubt everything and find your own light."- Buddha

That's All for Now!

How are you going to make sure you get the most from this book?

I would suggest going back through it. Maybe read one key a day and commit it to memory. Put it on a sticky note and stick it on your mirror where you'll be sure to see it.

Let the key run through your mind all day long so that it gets embedded and becomes a part of your working knowledge.

And if you found this helpful, pass it on! Share with your friends, family or colleagues.

If you've enjoyed this book and have gotten a lot out of it, stay in touch!

Visit www.LisaMeisels.com to find out more or send an inquiry to Lisa@LisaMeisels.com.

I love hearing from you!

Acknowledgments

I deeply acknowledge my husband Ken Meisels, who has always been there for me to lift me up and never questioned my ability to become successful from the moment we met.

To my daughter Acacia Bravo and my son Christian Bravo for always trusting in me. A huge thanks to my mom for opening my eyes to faith and choice, to my sister who has always believed in me and to my friends Moe Rush who always boosted my confidence and Victoria Imrie who jumped into the online business journey with me.

I want to thank my Awesome Out of The Box Goddess sisters Michelle Walker, Jennifer Russell and Sally Page who always encouraged me without judgement. To Madgie Avery who stood by my virtual side helping me get comfortable on camera. I want to thank the one coach who helped me feel seen for being me, Jennifer Darling. I thank my corporate bosses Kelly Selman and Lori Holland for believing in me and supporting my ability to mentor and train.

I have deep gratitude to all the thought leaders who have guided me on my spiritual journey and to my personal mentors Jennifer Darling, Ann Strout, Amber McLean, Matthew Pollard, Rob Goyette, Kristin Thompson, Maleah Jacobs, April and Ajay Matta, Jennifer McLean and Vrinda Normand's team who have supported me in growing my online business.

I want to express sincere gratitude to my spiritual mentor Angelica Rose, to Jill Hendrickson's guidance on writing this book and to all my animals who have been my constant companions.

Notes

Notes

Notes

Notes

Notes

Notes

Notes

Notes